DREAM INTERPRETATION
Handbook

FOR CHRISTIANS
Dictionary of Common Dream Symbols Included

By Van Williams

Table of Contents

ACKNOWLEDGEMENTS

I want to give thanks to my Heavenly Father, the Most High God, "who saves the upright in heart" (Psalm 7:10). Thank you for sending your son Lord to redeem me, through his blood shed and the resurrection power. Thank you for saving me, forgiving me, cleansing me, training me, equipping me, and choosing me. I love you and I'm honored to be a child of the King of Kings and Lord of Lords.

I'm so grateful for your mercy being extended to me, and for the honor of being able to serve your people. My ultimate desire is to "run my race" well, and to please you Lord, in Jesus name. Amen.

I would also like to send a huge thank you, to my children whom the Lord has used as an extension of his own love towards me, for my mom who has shown me unconditional love and support. For all my loved ones, including my siblings, friends, leaders, mentors, and mentees, thank you for your support and believing in the call of God on my life, and the message the Lord has given me to proclaim.

I'm forever grateful.

INTRODUCTION

In "Dream Interpretation Handbook for Christians," Van Williams delves into the origin of dreams and visions. She offers a uniquely biblical perspective, revealing their true origins and significance. This insightful guide takes readers on a spiritual journey into the world of dreams, grounded in the wisdom of Scripture. Williams draws from the Bible, emphasizing stories of key dreamers like Joseph and Daniel. She skillfully helps believers distinguish between various dream types, from prophetic revelations to symbolic riddles. The book empowers readers to interpret dreams with discernment and an open heart, nurturing a deeper connection with God and a heightened understanding of His divine communication.

"Dream Interpretation Handbook for Christians" is an essential resource for those seeking spiritual growth and a closer faith journey. Van Williams' blend of biblical insight and practical guidance promises clarity, spiritual enlightenment, and a profound sense of purpose.

CHAPTER 1-
THE OVERVIEW OF DREAMS AND WHY WE HAVE THEM

Throughout history, the Lord has communicated with both believers and nonbelievers through the realm of dreams. Considering that we spend about one-third of our lives asleep, it is logical to assume that the Lord would use this time for communication with His creation. This chapter explores the reasons behind our dreams, delves into the history of dream interpretation, examines the various types of dreams for believers in Christ, and helps you understand the biblical context of the Lord speaking to His children.

Through foundational teaching, we'll discuss common dream types and share tips for improving sleep and experiencing what I refer to as "prophetic dreams." This chapter aims to provide a comprehensive understanding of heaven's language through the lens of dreams.

Reference: Sleephealth.org, "The State of Sleep Health in America in 2022"

The scripture in Job 33:14-18 tells us, "For God does speak, now one way now another, though no one perceives it. In a dream, in a vision of the night when deep sleep falls on people, as they slumber in their beds, he may speak in their ears and terrify them with warnings, to turn them from wrongdoing and keep them from pride, to preserve them from the pit, their lives from perishing by the sword."

I appreciate how this verse confirms that the Lord communicates with us through dreams, highlighting that many may not recognize the importance of their dreams. They don't "perceive it" as a message from the Lord. In my own case study as a minister of the Gospel, I've asked people I minister to if they were aware that the Lord speaks through dreams. Only about 50% knew, and just 1% could understand the meaning of their dreams.

This case study motivated me to help people understand the language of heaven. I started teaching on this subject because I believe recognizing and understanding dreams can be transformative. Picture this: the Lord inviting you into a conversation through a dream. As the scripture teaches, God sends us dreams to warn and preserve us. Our dreams unveil even the hidden aspects of our subconscious that God wants us to address.

The History of Dream Interpretation in Christianity

Throughout biblical history, the Lord has consistently communicated through the realm of dreams to provide correction, warnings, reveal divine purpose, and offer comfort. While there are numerous instances of people receiving prophetic dreams, the Bible specifically mentions only two men skilled in dream interpretation.

The first man, Joseph, renowned for his ability in dream interpretation, demonstrated his skill in Genesis chapter 40 while in prison. Two men troubled by their dreams sought Joseph's insight, and he, possessing the wisdom of the Lord, accurately interpreted their dreams. This example underscores that not everyone had the proficiency to interpret dreams, but Joseph did.

Another illustration comes from the book of Daniel, where the prophet is noted for understanding dreams and visions of all kinds (see Daniel 1:17). Both Joseph and Daniel were recognized for their expertise in dream interpretation, reflecting their possession of the Lord's wisdom.

As with any skill in life, proficiency comes through cultivation. I believe these two men, carrying the spirit of the Lord, became skilled by stewarding their dreams and seeking understanding from the Lord.

My prayer is that, just as Joseph and Daniel stewarded their dreams well and became skilled in dream interpretation, you too will cultivate this ability.

Spiritual Association Dreams

As mentioned in previous chapters, the Lord has consistently communicated through dreams to both believers and unbelievers. However, there is a distinction in the types of dreams and visions received by believers compared to unbelievers. Throughout scripture, the Lord has sent numerous dreams to both these groups. For instance, in Genesis 31:24, the Lord warned Laban, an idol worshiper, in a dream, advising him not to say anything to his son Jacob. Typically, the Lord sends dreams to unbelievers, offering them an opportunity to repent.

Believers, too, encounter dreams designed to lead them to repentance, along with other types of dreams and spiritual experiences. In Joel 2:28, the Lord, through the Prophet Joel, declared, "I will pour out my Spirit on all people. Your sons and daughters will prophesy, your old men will dream dreams, your young men will see visions."

As children of God, the Lord has ordained that we, as His followers, would receive the Holy Spirit "poured out" into us, leading us to "dream dreams and see visions." This prophecy foretells that dreams and visions are connected to a spiritual experience from the Lord.

Divine messages

When encountering a divine message in a dream, I've observed, both from my personal experiences and the examples in the Bible, that a message from the Lord is firmly imprinted in your memory. Upon waking from such a dream, you often find it impossible to forget what you saw. Even if the meaning is unclear, there's usually an inner "knowing" that recognizes the dream as a divine message.

As Jesus states in John 10, "My sheep know my voice." Therefore, as believers, when recalling our dreams, we discern the voice of God.

Visions of the future

Depending on an individual's spiritual gifts, they might possess the gift of prophecy as outlined in 1 Corinthians 12. This prophetic grace often enables individuals to witness future events revealed through dreams. The Lord may grant someone a dream or vision regarding something to come, prompting them to pray or speak about it. This event might involve another individual, or the Lord may simply want to inform the person about what lies ahead. Amos 3:7 reminds us, "Surely the Sovereign Lord does nothing without revealing his plans to his servants the prophets" (NIV). Depending on your spiritual gifting, the Lord may unveil His plans to you before they unfold.

Communicating with spirits

Frequently, we experience encounters in our dreams involving interactions with spiritual beings, including ministering angels. Conversely, there are instances where we may encounter demons, referred to as fallen angels in Revelation 12:9.

Numerous examples in scripture depict spiritual beings appearing in various forms, often taking on a human appearance. In Genesis 19, the Bible recounts how angels, appearing as men, went to Lot's house to save him.

Even when Satan is described in Isaiah 14:16, the depiction is in the form of a man. It's crucial to pay attention to the context of the dream and your emotions because these dreams often involve communion with the Holy Spirit, angelic beings, and at times, reveal the plans of the enemy.

Types of Dreams and their Place in Christianity

The scriptures offer numerous examples of different dream types to enhance our understanding of our own dreams. As mentioned earlier in this chapter, we encounter many dreams designed to lead us to repentance. Additionally, the Lord imparts what I refer to as covenant dreams, unveiling His promises for our lives. For instance, in a dream (Genesis 15), the Lord promised Abraham that he would become a nation with numerous offspring.

Another category involves dreams of deliverance. In these dreams, we may experience deliverance. Peter, for example, had a vision where he observed various types of animals and heard a voice instructing him to "Get up, Peter. Kill and eat" (Acts 10:13-14). The Lord conveyed to Peter not to deem impure what God had made clean. The revelation in the dream aimed to deliver Peter from discrimination and adherence to tradition. I once had a dream of impartation where Jesus bestowed spiritual gifts upon my hands, and upon waking up, I still felt the power of that experience.

A variety of dream types exists, and some of the most common ones we'll discuss next include prophetic dreams, recurring dreams, lucid dreams, vivid dreams, and nightmares.

Prophetic Dreams:

Prophetic dreams involve the Holy Spirit revealing information to the dreamer.
In such dreams, the dreamer may witness future events, receive accurate knowledge, or gain foresight about an individual or situation. The Lord might also disclose details to the dreamer regarding future events concerning their own life. Typically, these dreams are bestowed upon individuals according to their gifting. As Amos 3:7 states, "Surely the Lord God does nothing without revealing to his servants the prophets." If you possess the gift of prophecy or have a prophetic gifting, you are likely to receive these types of dreams more frequently than those without such gifts.

Recurring Dreams:

 When it comes to recurring dreams, seeing a dream more than once suggests that the Lord is trying to convey one of two things. The first reason for experiencing a recurring dream may be due to not fully grasping the message or the depth of what God was communicating within the dream. In such cases, a lack of appropriate response prompts God to emphasize urgency and prompt attention.

 Another reason for recurring dreams could be that the Lord has decisively determined a matter. As Joseph explained to Pharaoh in Genesis 41:32, the repetition of two dreams with the same meaning indicated that the Lord had firmly decided that what was seen would happen soon.

Lucid Dreams:

According to the Oxford Language Dictionary, lucid dreams are experiences where an individual has a vivid awareness of being in a dream. I'll provide an example from my own encounter. The Lord warned me of the pandemic and divine opportunities. In January 2020, I dreamt that I was driving. Suddenly, the car accelerated uncontrollably, and despite my attempts to slow down, the brakes failed. I found myself in a field surrounded by parked planes, colliding with them one by one. Gripping the wheel, I couldn't regain control. Power lines started falling, a whirlwind of "dust" filled the air, and crowds of people were in chaos. As a power line descended onto my car's hood, panic set in. Terrified, I thought it would destroy me. In that moment, I realized it was a dream, a message from the Lord, bringing me peace thereafter.

The Lord conveyed that He was accelerating my life beyond my control (hence the plane crashes and inability to slow down). He also revealed there would be a significant economic downturn and chaos among the people, symbolized by the "crash" and the "dust in the air."

In hindsight, I recognize this lucid, vivid dream as the Lord foretelling the global pandemic and COVID.

Nightmares:

Surprisingly, night terrors can originate from both the Lord and the demonic realm. Job 33 highlights that God communicates through dreams and visions, even if the dreamer isn't consciously aware. It states, "He may speak into their ears and terrify them with warnings" (Job 33:16). Often, the alarming dreams are the Lord's urgent warnings meant to safeguard us. Ephesians 6:12 reminds us that our struggle is not against flesh and blood but against the powers of darkness and spiritual forces of evil in heavenly realms.

In essence, your night terror serves as the Lord's way of revealing the enemy's plan against you, prompting you to engage in fervent prayer.

What influences the way you dream?

Various factors shape the way we dream and the quality of those dreams. If the dreamer is a Christian, a child of God, the dreams are tailored to provide guidance and instruction. Beyond faith, lifestyle and daily habits significantly impact the nature of dreams and what the Lord may reveal.

Character trust is crucial. Can the Lord trust you with sensitive information? If He discloses secrets or insights about others, can He rely on your integrity, love, and commitment to prayer?

External factors like alcohol consumption, medication, or impairments during waking hours can influence dream content.

Entertainment choices play a role in dream quality. Consider the movies, music, and spiritual engagement, such as Bible study. The prefix for entertainment is "enter," emphasizing that what enters our eyes and ears shapes our spirit – either strengthening it or causing spiritual dullness, affecting our dreams.

Life circumstances, like worries, may manifest in the subconscious, giving rise to what I term "soul-ish" dreams.

Tips and Tricks for Enhancing Your Sleep and Dreams:

In this section, I want to offer you a few tips that I believe will help improve your ability to "dream dreams" and "see visions" (Joel 2:28).

Tip Number 1: A key to experiencing more quality dreams is by meditating on the word of God.
John 1:1 says, "In the beginning was the Word, and the Word was with God, and the Word was God." Jesus is that "Word." The more we meditate on the word, the more we begin to reflect the character of Jesus, our Lord.
Psalm 119:130 says, "The entrance of thy words giveth light."

Tip Number 2: Maintain a consistent prayer life. Prayer is a conversation with the heavenly Father. The more you communicate with Him, the more He communicates with you.

Tip Number 3: Demonstrate stewardship over your dreams by documenting them upon waking up and seeking the Lord for their interpretation.
"He gives wisdom to the wise" (Daniel 2:21). In this context, when you're intentional about stewarding your dreams, the Lord will trust that He can speak to you more frequently through dreams, as He did with others throughout the Bible.

Tip Number 4: Adequate rest is crucial for receiving quality dreams from heaven. "Truly my soul finds rest in God" (Psalm 62:1). "He grants sleep to those he loves" (Psalm 127:2). The Lord desires that we are fully rested so that our souls are at peace. Our soul encompasses our mind, will, and emotions. When we have calmness in those areas, it becomes easier for us to discern the Lord, even through our dreams.

How dreams can strengthen your faith:

I can attest that, from personal experiences, receiving messages from God through dreams has transformed my life, taking my faith to another dimension. Through dreams and visions, the Lord revealed my identity in Him and His perfect will for my life, even before I fully submitted to His ways. He showed me a version of myself I would've never believed possible.

Years ago, the Lord revealed through a dream that I was born a Prophet, His "mouthpiece," increasing my faith. In subsequent dreams, He declared my promotion to be His Apostle, commissioning me for His work. These dreams fueled my faith and led me to start a ministry.

This passion drives my commitment to teaching the importance of dreaming and stewarding them well, as they have radically shaped my life. I believe that if the Lord could bless me through dreams, He can certainly do the same for you.

I've received counsel and strategy through dreams related to business, relationships, etc. The messages in our dreams can be literal or symbolic, often presented in parabolic language—stories and metaphors. Just as Jesus spoke to His disciples in parables, these messages invite us to draw closer to the Lord for a deeper understanding of His mysteries.

Key Takeaways:

 Understanding the language of Heaven and interpreting dreams starts with receiving foundational teaching on the biblical history of dreams. The Bible tells us, "You will know the truth, and the truth shall set you free" (John 8:32).

 Knowing these "truths" about dreams being a language from heaven opens individuals to receive more, motivating the Lord to reveal further. The chapter covers:

 1. Defining dreams and exploring their purpose.
 2. Recognizing that the Lord communicates through dreams, impacting both believers and unbelievers, encouraging repentance and preserving lives.

 Additionally, the chapter explores the history of dream interpretation, highlighting the proficiency of figures like Daniel and Joseph. It emphasizes that by cultivating our gifts, we can become skilled interpreters. Common dream types such as Prophetic dreams, recurring dreams, lucid/vivid dreams, and nightmares are discussed.

 Finally, the chapter provides four practical tips for dreamers to implement, enhancing the overall quality of their dreams.

CHAPTER 2:
UNDERSTANDING DREAMS THROUGH GOD'S WORD

Imagine, for a moment, the Lord Jesus—the Son of the living God, the creator of the universe and everything within it—taking a moment of His time to converse with you. This is the most profound way I can convey the significance of receiving a dream. The Lord engages in conversation through images while we rest, using dreams to reveal what He needs us to know. Hence, it is vital for us to seek understanding regarding the meaning of our dreams and not dismiss them casually.

Throughout this chapter, I will share the benefits of dreams, how dreams are interpreted based on biblical history, and some noteworthy dreams in the Bible. This will provide you with a deeper understanding of how to discern the word through your dreams and interpret them more skillfully.

How dreams can benefit your faith

 I appreciate how the Lord, through His Holy Spirit, provides the comfort needed to strengthen our faith. Many dreams have revealed promises, deepening my trust in God. One dream, particularly impactful during a tough season, came from my then 5-year-old daughter. In the midst of challenging times, the Lord warned me through her dream about an upcoming and necessary testing. Despite the difficulty, dealing with loss and weariness, her dream provided unexpected encouragement. In it, she witnessed being taken to heaven, observing Jesus placing a crown on my head, signifying my "certificate." He gave me a large key and a sword, commanding me to "preach the gospel now." This dream significantly boosted my confidence when I needed it most. It highlights the power of dreams to enhance our faith and belief in God, regardless of the circumstances.

Dreams can help you learn:

From my personal experience, I've discovered that the Lord sends us dreams to reinforce lessons. A memorable dream from years ago stands out vividly. On a rock, I conversed with my uncle, symbolizing the Holy Spirit. Expressing my desire to learn how to minister, he shared a parable. "A woman stopped getting water directly from the lake, and her water became impure." The lesson was clear: seek God's voice and instruction directly, even though learning from others is valuable.

Dreams can enhance creativity

As mentioned in a previous section, dreams from the Lord can offer significant benefits, playing a crucial role in providing dreamers with creative strategies for achieving prosperity. Yes, your dream could unveil "witty ideas" that propel you to a higher financial bracket. A compelling example is found in Genesis 30-31 with Jacob.

In a dream, the Lord revealed to Jacob an innovative approach to facilitating animal mating, resulting in the production of spotted offspring. Jacob, facing wage deceit from his employer Laban, received this strategy from God. Laban, skeptical of the plan, agreed to let Jacob keep all the spotted animals. Implementing the dream's strategy, Jacob accumulated wealth through the newfound ownership of numerous spotted livestock.

Dreams can be therapeutic

The Bible refers to the Holy Spirit as our comforter in John 14:26. Even in our dreams, the Holy Spirit provides comfort, often creating a "therapeutic" experience. In my dream interpretation classes, I guide students in understanding that the Lord may reveal Himself in a dream as a trusted ministry leader, whether personally known or not. The Holy Spirit might appear as a parent, teacher, or best friend, delivering a timely message, perhaps a reassuring "I am with you." Often, the dream conveys the peaceful presence of God, offering the comfort needed for that individual.

How dreams are interpreted in the bible

Throughout biblical history, the Lord has consistently communicated with humanity through dreams, as promised in Joel 2:28: "And afterward, I will pour out my Spirit on all people. Your sons and daughters will prophesy, your old men will dream dreams, your young men will see visions." Dreams and visions have always been the Lord's means of conveying messages to His people.

Examining the birth and arrival of Jesus Christ, we find that the Lord's will was unveiled through dreams. Consider Mary, pledged to be married to Joseph. After an angel revealed to her about Jesus and she became pregnant through the Holy Spirit (Matthew 1), Joseph, unaware of the divine conception, planned to divorce her quietly. In a pivotal dream, an angel directed Joseph to take Mary as his wife and name the baby Jesus, who would become the savior. Thus, the Lord used a dream to ensure the coming of Christ.

The Lord continued to reveal His plans through the earthly parents of Jesus. In another crucial dream, an angel warned Joseph about King Herod's threat to baby Jesus's life. Instructed through the dream, Joseph took his family to Egypt, preserving the life of Jesus.

Joseph, the Interpreter of Dreams

There's another man in the Bible named Joseph who not only frequently received dreams from the Lord but also gained a reputation for interpreting various kinds of dreams. I find Joseph's story and life fascinating because it vividly illustrates how dreams can profoundly influence an individual's life and direction.

At the age of 17, Joseph had two distinct dreams that he shared with his brothers and parents. These dreams revealed his future leadership over his family and his elevation to the point where they would "bow down" to him. Unfortunately, sharing these dreams led to increased hatred from his brothers, who plotted to kill him but ended up selling him into slavery in Egypt. One crucial lesson here is the importance of discernment in choosing whom to share our dreams with— not every dream is meant for everyone.

Fast forward, Joseph found himself in prison nearly 20 years later, where he encountered two fellow prisoners with disturbing dreams. Joseph correctly interpreted the dreams, prophesying that one would be killed in three days, and the other would be reinstated as the cupbearer to the king within the same timeframe. About two years later, when Pharaoh had perplexing dreams, the cupbearer recommended Joseph to the king, citing his skill in dream interpretation.

Consequently, Joseph interpreted Pharaoh's dream, leading to his release from prison. Due to his exceptional wisdom and connection with the Holy Spirit, Joseph was elevated to second in command, overseeing all of Egypt.

Significant Dreams in the Bible

The dreams sent by the Lord to Pharaoh in Genesis 41 served as warnings about future events, enabling him to position himself to protect the nation through preparation.

The Lord presented two distinct dreams to Pharaoh. In the first dream, Pharaoh stood by the Nile, witnessing seven fat cows emerging from the river, followed by seven skinny cows that swallowed the fat ones. The second dream involved seven plump, healthy heads of grain growing from a single stalk, later consumed by seven thin, withered heads of grain.
Joseph explained to Pharaoh that these dreams were "one and the same" (Genesis 41:25), conveying a consistent message. The seven fat cows and the plump, healthy heads of grain symbolized seven years of abundance. Conversely, the seven skinny cows and the withered heads of grain swallowing the previous abundance represented seven years of famine following the plentiful years. Remarkably, the Lord communicated a warning dream to an unbeliever, Pharaoh, for the preservation of his people.

Daniel's Four Beasts

Another significant dream in the Bible was experienced by the Prophet Daniel. In this particular vision, he witnessed four beasts emerging from the sea. The first resembled a lion with wings like an eagle. Daniel described its wings being torn off, and it stood upright like a human on two feet. This beast was immensely powerful, terrifying, possessing the mind of a human.

The second beast resembled a bear and was instructed to "get up and eat your fill of flesh" (Daniel 7:5). The third had the appearance of a leopard with four wings like a bird, four heads, and the authority to rule. The fourth beast was powerful and large with iron teeth and ten horns. The horns had eyes, and one, in particular, spoke boastfully.

These four beasts symbolized four distinct kingdoms that would rise from various regions on Earth. As we progress through the chapter, all the beasts eventually lost their authority as the "Ancient of Days" emerged. Our Lord was granted all authority and dominion over everything.

Abimelek's Warning

Another notable dream involving a divine rebuke and warning occurred in Genesis 20. This dream was sent to a man named Abimelek, who served as the king of Gerar.

At that time, our patriarch Abraham and his wife Sarah were traveling through this region. Fearing for his life due to Sarah's beauty, Abraham misled Abimelek, stating that Sarah was his sister. Abraham worried that the king might desire his wife and, in turn, harm him.

In response, the Lord appeared to Abimelek, who was an unbeliever, warning him that he was "as good as dead" unless he returned Sarah to her husband. The following morning, the king returned Sarah to Abraham and even bestowed blessings upon the Prophet Abraham for the unintentional wrongdoing.

Jacob's Ladder

In Genesis 28, a man named Jacob had his first recorded encounter with the Lord in Scripture. While resting in a place called Bethel, with his head resting on a stone, Jacob had a dream. In this dream, he saw a stairway extending from heaven to earth, with angels "ascending and descending" upon it. The Lord then appeared to Jacob, identifying Himself as the God of his forefathers, Abraham and Isaac.

During this encounter, the Lord established a covenant with Jacob, assuring him of His presence and promising numerous descendants. Within the dream, the Lord revealed His plans for Jacob's offspring and assured him of His continual watchful care, no matter where Jacob went.

Laban's Warnings

Another significant dream in the Bible involving an unbeliever occurred with a man named Laban, who happened to be Jacob's father-in-law. Jacob, who worked for Laban, faced constant deceit in his wages.

In Genesis 31, following God's instruction, Jacob decided to discreetly leave, taking all his possessions, including his wives and children, without Laban's knowledge. When Laban discovered their departure, he pursued them. In a dream, the Lord came to Laban and cautioned him, saying, "Be careful not to say anything bad to Jacob, good or bad." It's notable how the Lord, through this dream, warned Laban about his interactions with Jacob, providing reassurance that the Lord defends His children.

Nebuchadnezzar's Statue

 In the book of Daniel, there reigned a wicked king named Nebuchadnezzar over Babylon during the time when Daniel, the prophet, served in the palace as a wise man.

 The king had a dream that, according to the Bible, none of the wise men, enchanters, magicians, or diviners could interpret under the penalty of death. Seeking revelation from God, the prophet Daniel was shown by the Lord that the king had seen "an enormous statue, with a head made of gold, chest and arms of silver, belly and thighs of bronze, legs of iron, and feet of iron and baked clay." In the dream, a rock was cut out, struck the statue's feet, breaking it into pieces that were then swept away by the wind. The rock that struck the statue became a large mountain and filled the Earth.

 The Lord's interpretation revealed that the rock, symbolizing the kingdom of God, would soon crush all other kingdoms represented by the various materials (gold, silver, bronze, iron, and clay) in the statue.

The Wisdom of Solomon

One of my personal favorite biblical dreams involves a man named Solomon, who became king in place of his father, David. After Solomon made a substantial sacrifice to the Lord, God appeared to him in a dream.

"At Gibeon, the Lord appeared to Solomon during the night in a dream, and God said, 'Ask for whatever you want me to give you' (1 Kings 3:5)." Solomon's response to the Lord was, "Give your servant a discerning heart to govern your people and to distinguish between right and wrong" (1 Kings 3:9).

The Lord, pleased with Solomon's request that did not seek personal wealth, long life, or harm to his enemies, promised Solomon wisdom, honor, wealth, and a legacy unparalleled by any other kings.

Hearing God's Word in Dreams

There are various examples in scripture that illustrate the diverse ways the Lord can reveal Himself to us, even within our dreams. We observe instances where the Lord communicates with both devoted followers and those who might be considered unbelievers. Notably, many dreams given to unbelievers serve as warnings, such as in the case of King Nebuchadnezzar's dream with the statue, allowing God to affirm His status as the one true God. These dreams provide an opportunity for unbelievers to seek out the voice of God, even through His prophets.

Throughout history, the Lord has used dreams to connect with believers, addressing our day-to-day concerns. While the Bible remains our primary source for seeking God's voice and receiving His word, the beauty of God imparting dreams to His followers lies in the personalized nature of His guidance within the dream.

A crucial aspect in ensuring that a dream is from God is recognizing that it will never contradict His word. If a dream goes against the Word of God, it's essential to pray against deception. Since God alone can reveal mysteries, seeking His insight through prayer is paramount.

How to Interpret Dreams Through Faith

I share a few tips on interpreting dreams, particularly for Christian believers. It's crucial to remember that if you're a believer in Christ, the Lord will never instruct you, even in a dream, to do anything contrary to His own word.

I've observed that some dreams even depict actual Bible verses. For instance, in one dream, a lit path I was driving on led to scenes of leaping over buildings and scaling a wall, leaving enemies defeated. When I explored the scripture for references to "light" or "lamp," I found guidance in 2 Samuel 22:29-30: "You, Lord, are my lamp; the Lord turns my darkness into light. With your help, I can advance against a troop; with my God, I can scale a wall." The Lord conveyed this message to me through the dream, emphasizing the importance of seeking scripture for understanding symbols in dreams.

Identify Your Emotions

Another tip I suggest is to be attentive to your emotions within the dream. Surprisingly, this aspect can provide significant insight into what the Lord might be communicating to you. Take note of whether you felt happy, sad, angry, afraid, or uncertain, and document these emotions along with the dream details upon waking up. Considering the context of the dream, ask yourself, "In what part of your life are you experiencing similar emotions?" The Lord may be using the dream to address a situation in your life that evokes those specific emotions.

Assign meanings to the Details

The Lord communicates with us based on our existing knowledge and how we interpret information. This explains why certain symbols may hold different meanings for different individuals. For instance, a dream featuring a dog might carry a negative connotation for someone who dislikes dogs, while it could be positive for someone who loves them.

A helpful tip I share with my students that has proven effective in dream interpretation is to write down your dreams. As you delve into the dream's details, note what different symbols mean to you. Consider the overall context of the dream and your emotions during it. Finally, seek clarity from the Lord, asking Him to make the message clear.

Literal Versus Symbolic Interpretations of Dreams

Understanding that not every dream conveys a literal message is crucial; many dreams tend to be more symbolic than literal, requiring followers of Christ to rely on the Lord and seek His guidance.

Joseph's statement in Genesis 40:8, "Do not interpretations belong to God?" and Daniel's mention in Daniel 2:28, "But there is a God in Heaven who reveals mysteries," emphasize that interpretation ultimately comes from the Lord. Even if we follow tips from others, it is God who clarifies a dream's meaning. The confirmation within your spirit acts as the Lord's assurance.

Common concerns in dreams often involve themes of death. It's essential to understand that dreams of death are usually symbolic, signaling the end of a situation rather than a literal death.

Another common concern arises when the dreamer engages in sinful actions contrary to their waking behavior. Such dreams may indicate demonic presence aiming to lead the dreamer into agreement with an evil plan. Upon waking, it's advisable to pray against the enemy's plans, canceling them in Jesus' name.

Common Dream Tropes for Christians

It's crucial to acknowledge that the Lord communicates with individuals based on their unique capacities. While common dream types exist among most Christians, the interpretation of symbols can vary depending on personal experiences and beliefs. The Lord takes these individual nuances into account when conveying messages through dreams.

A vivid example is a dream my daughter had. In the dream, a classmate mentioned to her that he was transferring to a school, which for the sake of being anonymous, I'll refer to it as "ABC school". In the dream, she began to feel sad when this student made that statement and instantly got sad. The next scene of the dream, a little boy was crouched under a bench and yelled out the same statement, "I'm going to ABC school". Upon her waking up and sharing the dream, I was able to understand her emotions, through Holy Spirit's guidance and I realized that "ABC school" held significance for her, representing an experience of someone she knew who battled depression and suicidal thoughts. This insight led to the interpretation that the Lord was urging her to pray for that classmate in the dream who was dealing with depression. This example illustrates how personal experiences contribute to dream interpretation.

Flying

Many dreamers have encountered the sensation of flying within their dreams, and based on my experience, this can often indicate the presence of witchcraft within the individual's bloodline. If you experience this, it may be an opportunity to seek deliverance, specifically renouncing any connection to witchcraft stemming from either personal sins or ancestral transgressions. The enemy might try to initiate individuals into an unholy destiny or impart evil gifts through such dreams.

However, if you find yourself being lifted up in the air, not necessarily flying, it could signify a prophetic gifting from the Lord. This lifting could symbolize the Lord granting you a perspective from a higher dimension, allowing you to perceive beyond what is typically accessible to most.

Falling:

When a dreamer experiences a fall in their dream, it typically signifies a form of failure in a specific area of their life. It's important to pay attention to the context of the dream – what were you doing when you fell, and how did the fall make you feel? The Lord may be addressing an area where things seem unsuccessful for the dreamer.

Depending on the dream's details, the Lord could be conveying a message of encouragement or issuing a warning. Proverbs 24:16 reinforces that "the righteous fall seven times, they rise again, but the wicked stumble when calamity strikes.

Dying:
Dreams depicting death are typically symbolic rather than literal. In scripture, death carries various meanings. Proverbs 6:23 highlights that "the wages of sin is death, but the gift of God is eternal life in Christ Jesus our Lord."

 The context of the dream is crucial, as death in a dream may serve as a warning from the Lord, signaling the need for correction or repentance by the dreamer. Apostle Paul also noted that "our old self was crucified with Christ." Often, the symbolism of "death" in a dream signifies the conclusion of one season and the transition into something new, or the cessation of an old sinful lifestyle and the embrace of a new life in Christ.

Teeth:
 Teeth are often symbolic of wisdom in dreams. If a person has missing teeth in a dream, it may suggest that the Lord is indicating a lack of wisdom in a specific area, aiming to provide guidance for seeking necessary counsel. False teeth within a dream could symbolize misinformation or false knowledge regarding a matter.

 Wearing braces in a dream indicates personal growth in wisdom and understanding. Similar to braces in the natural world that align teeth correctly, the dreamer wearing braces is undergoing a similar process of alignment and growth in wisdom.

Types of Symbols in Dreams

Encountering various symbols in dreams, such as animals, people, objects, or specific locations, is common. Recognizing and defining these symbols within the dream is a crucial step in dream interpretation. Seeking the guidance of God's Word is essential to understanding what these symbols mean. While personal feelings about a symbol may differ from God's perspective, Isaiah 55:8 reminds us that His thoughts are beyond ours.

To interpret symbols, it's advisable to compare them with biblical references and consider the context of the dream's message. If a symbol isn't explicitly mentioned in the Bible, a practical approach is to reflect on its meaning in the natural realm. For instance, seeing a notebook and pen may signify the need to "take note" of something important, requiring attention to specific details.

Animals:

Animals have consistently played a symbolic role in our dreams, extending back to biblical times. Each animal within a dream typically carries distinct meanings. In Genesis 41, for instance, Pharaoh's dream featured cows symbolizing the financial state of the nation, reflecting the prevalent livestock during that period.

Lions, often associated with the "Lion of the Tribe of Judah," represent Jesus and carry symbolic significance related to Apostolic grace—the role of a pioneer or builder. Additionally, scripture references lions as a metaphor for Satan, described as one who "prowls around like a roaring lion, seeking whom he may devour" (1 Peter 5:8). Always consider the dream's context for accurate interpretation.

Objects:

Concerning objects within a dream, the dreamer should initially contemplate the natural function of the object. Take an ID card, for instance; its primary purpose is to identify and verify essential details about an individual. If, in a dream, your ID card goes missing, it might signify a temporary loss of sight regarding your purpose or a hindrance by the enemy preventing you from operating fully in your calling.

My recommendation is, after understanding the object's natural function, connect it with other details in your dream to derive a comprehensive interpretation.

People:

People in dreams are often symbolic, representing someone or something else. While the Lord might convey a message about a specific person based on your gifting, it's crucial to recognize that, in many instances, people are symbolic.

For instance, a trusted ministry leader in a dream might symbolize the Holy Spirit. A best friend or a parent could convey a timely message from God. Supportive figures in your dream might signify angelic assistance, while deceitful individuals, including earthly enemies, might represent demons or Satan.

At times, the person in your dream embodies the meaning of their name. For instance, if someone named Destiny appears, the Lord could be communicating about your destiny.

Places:

Concerning places in dreams, some are symbolic, while others are literal. Take, for instance, the Apostle Paul's dream in Acts 16:9-10, where he envisioned a man in the town of Macedonia, pleading for a visit. Paul understood this dream as a literal instruction to preach the gospel to those people.

Dreaming of a childhood home is a common location, and its recurrence might signify something generational. The Lord could be addressing past issues to bring deliverance. The frequency of these dreams could also indicate setbacks in the dreamer's life.

Experiences:

The dreamer may encounter certain experiences that are typically symbolic. For instance, I've dreamed of being on a rocket, symbolizing my life "taking off" into the things of God.

Common experiences include being on an elevator or a staircase. If you're going up, it indicates elevation into God's plans. Conversely, going down could suggest spiritual decline, requiring the dreamer's vigilance and prayer. The crucial key is to observe feelings and connect the experience with waking life.

Growing closer to God through dreams

One of the most beneficial practices for every believer, especially to enhance dream interpretation skills, is to become a student of the Word. Meditate on God's Word and consider having a Bible concordance as a helpful reference for studying and searching symbols found in your dreams. This approach has proven helpful in my own life.

Regarding the types and frequency of dreams we receive, the Lord communicates based on our individual understanding. For instance, some may encounter angels in their natural form, while others may not due to a lack of knowledge concerning the ministry of angels in the Word of God.

The Lord speaks to His children in dreams because He cares about every aspect of our lives. His desire is to assist, bring comfort, and reveal things to us. Seeking Him is crucial, as the Bible instructs to "seek first the kingdom of God and His righteousness, and all these things will be added unto us" (Matthew 6:33). Seeking the Lord involves studying His Word, learning His character, and understanding who He is.

Moreover, the more we seek the Lord's face through His Word, the more He adds to us, including His Spirit of wisdom and understanding, along with the ability to interpret His voice through dreams.

Key Takeaway

As an overview, we discussed in this chapter:
1. How dreams can benefit your faith.
2. How dreams are interpreted in the Bible.
3. Hearing God's word in dreams.
4. Significant dreams in the Bible.
5. Common Dream tropes for Christians.

We've explored various examples throughout scripture that illustrate the different ways the Lord reveals Himself to us in our dreams.

We highlighted that the Lord communicates through dreams regarding our day-to-day concerns.

It was emphasized that most dreams are symbolic rather than literal, with the literal interpretation often depending on the dreamer's spiritual gifts.

We discussed that dreams about people are often symbolic, representing what that person signifies to the dreamer, similar to the symbolism in our dreams.

Lastly, we reinforced the idea that studying the Word of God contributes to becoming more skilled in dream interpretation.

CHAPTER 3: ANIMALS

In this chapter, we explore significant animals that might appear in your dreams, aiming to offer insights into the messages the Lord may convey to you. It's crucial to understand that the interpretations provided here offer a general understanding, not always an exact representation. Each dreamer receives unique messages, often reflecting their personal perspective of a symbol.

For instance, the meaning of an animal can vary for different individuals based on the context of their dreams. This chapter includes dictionary entries of common dream animals and their interpretations in relation to scripture.

Alligator - *Dreaming of an alligator indicates a level of pride either rising against the dreamer or a revelation from the Lord about the presence of a spirit of pride. This reptile symbolizes stubbornness, self-exaltation, and boastfulness.*

Recognized for their thick scaly skin, large heads, and wide mouths, typically inhabit waters. The Bible references sea creatures, as in Isaiah 27:1, stating that the Lord will punish with His sword, targeting Leviathan, the gliding and coiling serpent, the monster of the sea. Job 41:34 highlights that Leviathan "looks down on all that are haughty; it is king over all that are proud."

Ant - *The ant is significant in Christianity as being the image of wisdom and dedication. The scripture states: "Take a lesson from the ants, you lazybones. Learn from their ways and become wise!"- (Proverbs 6:6 NLT.)*

In the context of the ant being shown in the dream, the Lord is speaking to the dreamer about the need to gain wisdom, and/or to use wisdom for a particular situation

Bats - *This nocturnal creature is predominantly active in darkness, making it a symbol of wickedness. Spotting a bat in a dream reveals a period of spiritual warfare surrounding the dreamer, possibly indicating trials and hardship. A dream featuring bats serves as an urgent warning, prompting the dreamer to pray and make necessary intercession.*

Bees- *Bees symbolize teamwork, collaboration, diligence, and persistence despite their small size. Their hard work and unified approach in accomplishing tasks serve as an inspiration. If you see a bee in your dream, it could be the Lord encouraging you to network with others, emphasizing collaboration for success in areas such as business, ministry, family, or other concerns.*

Additionally, bees also represent small distractions that can enter one's life and cause pain, drawing a parallel to Deuteronomy 1:44, where the Amorites, like a swarm of bees, posed a challenge to be faced and overcome.

Bird *- Birds in dreams serve as messengers, conveying messages that can be either good or evil. Drawing from biblical history, birds have been used to bring messages of provision from the Lord. For instance, in 1 Kings 17:2-4, the Lord commanded ravens to bring food to Elijah, who was hiding by the brook. Another example is Noah sending a bird outside the ark in Genesis 8 to verify if the floodwaters had dried up.*

Bugs - *Considered a pest and an annoyance, a bug in a dream signals the dreamer to be vigilant about distractions that could impede productivity. These distractions may not always be obvious, presenting as minor, unforeseen circumstances deliberately sent by the enemy to cause annoyance and frustration.*

Much like a small, sometimes unnoticed bug, this adversary can be easily overlooked as a seemingly random occurrence. The enemy disguises itself and its malevolent plan, hoping the dreamer remains unaware until it's too late. Dreaming of a bug reveals what has been formed as a weapon against you by the adversary.

Butterfly- *The butterfly in a dream is an indication of a season of visibility for the dreamer. This is almost always a message sent to bring encouragement to the individual. In many cases, the Lord is informing the dreamer that He "makes everything beautiful in it's time" (Reference Ecclesiastes 3:11).*

Additionally, the butterfly reveals the completion of a specific process that the dreamer may have had to endure. This butterfly is sometimes a confirmation that the process of being "pruned" has or will be completed soon.

Cat - *Spotting a cat in a dream is the Lord's way of indicating that deception is at play. Specifically, encountering a black cat in the dream signifies the presence of witchcraft.*

It is advisable to be watchful, alert, and prayerful to avoid "avoidable conflicts" that may be sent to cause destruction in the dreamer's life. Stay vigilant to safeguard against potential harm and challenges.

Chameleon- *The revelation of this evil spirit in the dream points to a cunning demonic force that has concealed itself so discreetly that the dreamer might not always recognize the attack. The lizard in the dream possesses the characteristic of avoiding recognition and seeks to disguise itself within the personality of the dreamer. Stay discerning to unmask and address this subtle spiritual threat.*

Cow - *A dream featuring a cow serves as a representation of both livestock and the financial state of an individual. A healthy cow in the dream suggests prosperity and provision, while an unhealthy cow may convey a message about potential resource scarcity.*

In Christianity, the symbolism of a cow in a dream aligns with Genesis 41, where Pharaoh's dream illustrated the financial state of Egypt. The seven fat cows represented seven years of prosperity, contrasting with the seven skinny cows representing seven years of famine.

Dinosaur - *Encountering a dinosaur in a dream signals the presence of an ancient evil spirit, potentially operating in the dreamer's bloodline. The significance of the dreamer perceiving it as a dinosaur indicates that the Lord wants them to recognize the evil spirit hidden in their ancestral roots and foundation.*

If the dreamer observes these dinosaurs moving in the opposite direction, it signifies that the dreamer has received deliverance from these generational spirits. This symbolizes overcoming the influence of ancestral forces in their life.

Dog - *The Bible identifies the dog as an unclean spirit, embodying the spirit of lust and perversion. In Philippians 3:2 (NLT), caution is given about those who do evil, referred to as "dogs," who pervert the truth to mislead others.*

Interpreting the dream depends on your feelings towards dogs and the dream's context. Additionally, the dog could symbolize a friend, as the phrase "man's best friend" suggests, adding complexity to the dream's meaning.

Donkey- *This creature symbolizes the grace to endure, humility, and aligning with the things of God, as reflected in Mark 11:2-3 (NLT), "Go into that village over there," he told them. "As soon as you enter it, you will see a young donkey tied there that no one has ever ridden. Untie it and bring it here. If anyone asks, 'What are you doing?' just say, 'The Lord needs it and will return it soon.' Donkeys also denote provision, and in specific dream scenarios, they may represent something perceived as embarrassing or less favorable.*

Dove *-The dove is commonly depicted as a symbol of the Holy Spirit. If you see a dove in your dream, it signifies the Lord's presence, echoing the moment in Matthew 3:16 (NLT) when the Spirit descended like a dove during Jesus's baptism. The dove represents qualities such as gentleness, meekness, kindness, and humility.*

Dragon *- As per the Bible, the dragon is identified as the deceiver, representing Satan. Revelation 12:9 reveals, "This great dragon—the ancient serpent called the devil, or Satan, the one deceiving the whole world—was thrown down to the earth with all his angels."*

Encountering a dragon in a dream is a signal for the dreamer to urgently pray. This creature symbolizes opposition against the dreamer, emphasizing the need for spiritual vigilance.

Eagle - The eagle symbolizes boldness and strength, echoing Isaiah 40:31 (NLT), which states, "But those who trust in the Lord will find new strength. They will soar high on wings like eagles. They will run and not grow weary. They will walk and not faint." The message for the dreamer is to find encouragement and strength in Jesus's teachings.

Additionally, the eagle signifies the Prophetic mantle. Dreaming of an eagle may be the Lord advising the individual that they will carry a strong Prophetic grace, referencing the gift of prophecy in 1 Corinthians 12.

Elephant - The appearance of this animal in your dream unveils significant attributes in your character. If you see an elephant, the Lord is likely advising that these characteristics are essential. It suggests the need to cultivate "thick skin," signifying emotional stability and resistance to being easily moved by circumstances. The elephant represents confidence and stands out from the crowd. The large ears on the elephant also spiritually indicate the dreamer's ability to hear the Lord more clearly.

Frog - The Bible recounts in the book of Exodus a moment when the Lord imposed a curse on the Egyptians and their land. One of the curses involved the release of numerous frogs throughout Egypt: "If you refuse to let them go, I will send a plague of frogs on your whole country." (Exodus 8:2)

Observing a frog in a dream symbolizes an unclean spirit and might even indicate a curse being projected against the dreamer.

Fish - The scripture depicts fish as representing individuals who will receive salvation in Christ: "And Jesus said to them, 'Follow me, and I will make you become fishers of men.'" (Mark 1:17) This suggests that the dreamer may be called to evangelize and win souls for the kingdom of heaven, with the fish symbolizing new believers in Christ.

 Fish also symbolize supernatural provision from the Lord. As illustrated in John 21:5-6 (NLT), the story of catching fish emphasizes the abundance of blessings and provision when aligned with the divine direction.

Horse - The horse symbolizes status, influence, notoriety, strength, power, and might. In scripture, horses are emblematic of being prepared and equipped for battle: "And the armies which were in heaven followed him upon white horses, clothed in fine linen, white and clean." (Revelation 19:14 KJV)

Lion - Lions symbolize Jesus, described in scripture as the "Lion of the Tribe of Judah" (Revelation 5:5). The lion conveys qualities of boldness, courage, and, at times, signifies the Lord releasing an Apostolic grace on a person.

 The interpretation of the lion in a dream can vary. In certain instances, the lion is portrayed as the enemy, as indicated in 1 Peter 5:8, where the Bible states that the enemy "prowls around like a roaring lion, seeking whom he may devour."

Lamb - Observing the Lamb in a dream holds various meanings. The Bible frequently references Lord Jesus as the Lamb: "In a loud voice they were saying: 'Worthy is the Lamb, who was slain, to receive power and wealth and wisdom and strength and honor and glory and praise!'" (Revelation 5:12 NIV)

 For Christians, the lamb is significant, symbolizing sacrifice and purity: "After breakfast, Jesus asked Simon Peter, 'Simon son of John, do you love me more than these?' 'Yes, Lord,' Peter replied, 'you know I love you.' 'Then feed my lambs,' Jesus told him." (John 21:15 NLT)

Octopus - With its numerous arms, this wicked marine spirit is assaulting to the individual in various ways, simultaneously aiming to ensnare them and bring about failure, setbacks, and destruction.

Pig- The symbolism of a pig in the Christian faith signifies a sinful nature, representing sin as "missing the mark." If a pig is revealed in your dream, it may indicate the need for repentance. Repentance, defined as changing one's mind, is urged by the Lord to prevent stumbling and encourage a shift in perspective.

 In Mark 5:12 (NIV), demons beg Jesus to be sent into a herd of pigs. This biblical account underscores the symbolic association of pigs with sin, emphasizing the need for individuals to heed the warning and embrace repentance.

Rabbit- Pray against any spirit seeking to devour your provision, leading to poverty, insufficiency, and lack. The rabbit, by nature, consumes harvested items like vegetables and fresh crops. Encountering this animal in a dream reveals that your provision may be under attack, providing revelatory knowledge for your awareness.

Sheep - Sheep symbolize the family of believers in Christ. As stated in John 10:27, "My sheep listen to my voice; I know them, and they follow me." Observing a flock of sheep in a dream signifies the Lord addressing his believers and followers within the Christian faith.

 The presence of sheep may also hold significance for the dreamer's purpose and calling. It could indicate a calling to church ministry or another form of leadership, echoing Jesus' instruction to Peter in John 21:16 (NLT) to care for His sheep.

Snake - Encountering a snake in a dream may symbolize evil, deception, witchcraft, accusatory words, slander, or gossip. Stay vigilant and pray against manipulation and deception, recalling the serpent's role in deceiving Eve in Genesis 3.

 For the believer in Christ, take comfort in the empowering message that we have authority over our enemy. As stated in Luke 10:19 (NIV), "I have given you authority to trample on snakes and scorpions and to overcome all the power of the enemy; nothing will harm you."

Spider - *The presence of a spider in your dream signifies projected deception against you. Moreover, if you observe a spider web, exercise caution as it may be a symbol of entrapment intended to cause destruction.*

Tiger *- "But he was wounded for our transgressions, bruised for our iniquities; the chastisement of our peace was upon him, and with his stripes, we are healed." (Isaiah 53:5 ASV) Tigers, often recognized by their stripes, symbolize the authoritative power bestowed upon us through Jesus for deliverance, as indicated in the dream context.*

 Based on the context of the dream, a tiger could also represent an evil occultic power in operation.

Wolf *- The image of the wolf is spiritually referenced as an enemy disguising itself as an ally, lurking as a ferocious predator to bring deception into the life of the believer. Scripture warns to "Beware of false prophets who come to you in sheep's clothing but inwardly are ravening wolves." (~ Matthew 7:15)*

CHAPTER 4: OBJECTS

Dreams from heaven are many times disregarded and not perceived as divine messages. This is primarily due to the symbolism not being as clear. Because of the lack of clarity, an important message birthed through the dream can be easily dismissed; or worse, it can cause the meaning to be misinterpreted, leaving the dreamer confused and without direction.

What you'll find in this chapter, is a compilation of common symbols and its most common definition based on biblical interpretation of these symbols. The goal is to allow you this reference as a guide, so that you may become more skilled in interpreting your own dreams.

Airplane - *The dreaming of an airplane is significant to the dreamer experiencing an upcoming promotion or divine opportunity, which may show the plane "taking off". This could represent both a physical opportunity and even being elevated spiritually. Many times, the opportunities depicted by an airplane, is a representation of a large ministry, in some capacity. Airplanes are also indicators of a person being aligned with the plans of the Lord, especially if the plane is soaring.*

 In the event of a plane crashing, this could represent some sort of failure; or it could symbolize the ending of a phase or previous assignment.

Bed- *If the dreamer finds themselves in a bed while in the dream, this is the Lord's way of providing deeper and more intimate revelation. The bed represents a place of peace, comfort, agreement, and covenant.*

 Frequently, when people dream of a bed, the focus is often on those sharing the bed with them, leading to misconceptions about the dream's true meaning.

 Take note of the individuals on the bed; this signals the dreamer about potential agreements being formed. It's not uncommon to observe a trusted leader, family member, or friend on your bed, symbolizing a covenant and mutual agreement. Conversely, if someone perceived as an enemy is present, it might indicate finding peace even with adversaries.

In instances involving strangers or animals in the bed, it could signify spiritual warfare, with the enemy attempting to entice the dreamer into alignment with a demonic agenda. Be extremely discerning with this dream and the source of who is trying to make a covenant/alliance with you.

Bible *- A Bible in your dream conveys a message urging the dreamer to read and apply the word of God. If your name or picture is seen in the Bible, it signifies a divine calling to ministry, suggesting significant works will be accomplished through you.*

Books *- The appearance of books in the dream signifies the importance of reading and studying for a specific aspect of the dreamer's life. It indicates a need for knowledge and understanding, suggesting the dreamer should spend more time studying a particular subject or, possibly, delve deeper into the word of God through the Bible. As the scripture says, "Study to shew thyself approved unto God" (2 Timothy 2:15 KJV).*

Bread*- Bread is illustrated as being the Word of God. This symbol in a dream will speak specifically on our individual need for Jesus and to be nourished by the word of God.*

"For the bread of God is the bread that comes down from heaven and gives life to the world." (John 6:33 NIV)

"Then Jesus declared, "I am the bread of life. Whoever comes to me will never go hungry, and whoever believes in me will never be thirsty." (John 6:35 NIV)

Bush- The bush in the dream can symbolize various meanings, serving as a hiding place for either the dreamer or their enemy, Satan. The specific context of the dream, such as someone hiding in the bush or a vision of a bush, provides better clarity. Another interpretation is that the Lord may be calling the dreamer to a more intimate relationship and possibly commissioning them to walk in their purpose. Drawing from the example in Exodus, prior to Moses being called by God, he witnessed a bush on fire:

"There the angel of the Lord appeared to him in a blazing fire from the middle of a bush. Moses stared in amazement. Though the bush was engulfed in flames, it didn't burn up." (Exodus 3:2 NLT)

"When the Lord saw Moses coming to take a closer look, God called to him from the middle of the bush, "Moses! Moses!" "Here I am!" Moses replied." (Exodus 3:4 NLT)

Car- This symbol signifies the dreamer's journey, particularly in the realms of family, ministry, and business. The vehicle serves as the means to reach a specific destination. The key is to observe who is driving the vehicle in the dream, as this person represents the influence on the dreamer's decision-making regarding specific aspects of their journey, be it family, business, or ministry.

Needing to refuel the vehicle with gas or attending to its tires symbolizes the preparation required for the impending assignment.

Chain- *Dreaming of chains typically signifies some form of bondage, urging the dreamer toward deliverance. If the person in the dream is bound by chains, I recommend they undergo self-deliverance through strategic prayer and fasting. If possible, seek a trained, Holy Spirit-filled Christian minister experienced in deliverance to assist you in leading you through deliverance.*

If the chains are no longer on the person, it indicates that deliverance has taken place. The example from Acts 16:25-26, where Paul and Silas prayed and sang hymns, resulting in an earthquake that broke everyone's chains, illustrates the power of deliverance.

Clock - *The clock in a dream signifies divine timing, conveying the message that the time has arrived or is drawing near for something specific in the dreamer's life.*

If the dream involves being late or behind schedule, it warns that there's a risk of missing a divine appointment due to inadequate preparation.

Cross - *The cross stands as the quintessential symbol of the Christian faith. It represents Jesus' sacrificial death, crucified on the cross as a living sacrifice, and resurrected three days later for the redemption of all believers. (Ref. Matthew 27)*

When someone sees a cross in a dream, it serves as a call to fix their gaze upon Jesus, "the author and perfecter of our faith." (Ref. Hebrews 12:2).

Additionally, the cross may act as a reminder that believers are called to sacrifice personal desires and relinquish unpleasing habits, as stated in the Bible, to faithfully follow Jesus. "Then Jesus said to his disciples, 'Whoever wants to be my disciple must deny themselves and take up their cross and follow me.'" (Matthew 16:24 NIV)

Doll *- Frequently, a dream featuring a doll indicates attachment and a desire for security. If an adult dreamer carries a doll reminiscent of a child, it might signify a need for comfort. However, the manner in which the dreamer seeks comfort could be deemed inappropriate, especially considering their maturity level in the context of their Christian faith.*

Apostle Paul mentions this in 1 Corinthians 13:11: "When I was a child, I spoke and thought and reasoned as a child. But when I grew up, I put away childish things." The dream of the adult carrying a doll, is to bring awareness that you have areas within you that need to mature.

Doors*- The symbol of a door holds profound significance in Christianity. According to Revelations 3:8 and Isaiah 22:22, the Lord has the authority to open doors that no one can shut and vice versa. Seeing a door in a dream often signifies an upcoming opportunity, either divinely opened or closed by the Lord for the dreamer's benefit. The closure of a door could also indicate divine protection. The reassuring message is that, with faith, no opposition can hinder a door already ordained by God for the individual.*

Flowers- *Dreams of flowers convey a message of "beauty instead of ashes" (Isaiah 61:3) in the dreamer's life. Flowers symbolize blessings, favor, and divine provision from the Lord. Drawing inspiration from Matthew 6:28-30, the dream reflects the assurance that God's care for the dreamer surpasses even the splendor of Solomon.*

Food *– This symbol represents nourishment, particularly in acquiring knowledge. It signifies the dreamer's engagement with deeper revelations in God's Word and gaining wisdom in various life aspects. If the food doesn't seem appealing, it serves as a warning to be discerning about your sources of guidance. In the context of the dream, the distasteful food suggests the need for more enriching knowledge, as opposed to your current knowledge. Drawing inspiration from Apostle Paul's analogy in 1 Corinthians 3:1-2, solid food reflects maturity in understanding the teachings of Christ.*

Fruit *- Galatians 5 mentions the fruit of the spirit, which lists the characteristics we should have as Holy Spirit filled believers.*
 "But the fruit of the Spirit is love, joy, peace, forbearance, kindness, goodness, faithfulness, gentleness and self-control. Against such things there is no law."
 Galatians 5:22-23 NIV

 As it relates to your dream, was the fruit mouthwatering and delicious? Was it fresh or did it appear to be rotten or distasteful?
 The Bible references the term fruit as it pertains to believers "baring good fruit", which In other words, is us having the ability to show evidence of us being true disciples Christ Jesus.

 "By their fruit you will recognize them. Do people pick grapes from thorn bushes, or figs from thistles? Likewise, every good tree bears good fruit, but a bad tree bears bad fruit. A good tree cannot bear bad fruit, and a bad tree cannot bear good fruit."
 (Matthew 7:16-18 NIV)

Hammer - "Is not my word like fire," declares the Lord, "and like a hammer that breaks a rock in pieces?"
 (Jeremiah 23:29 NIV)

The hammer is a representation of the powerful word of God that breaks yokes and brings deliverance to the dreamer.

Honey - "If the Lord is pleased with us, he will lead us into that land, a land flowing with milk and honey, and will give it to us."
 (Numbers 14:8 NIV)

Honey has always been a symbolism of the Promises of God throughout the Bible. Seeing honey in the dream is the Lord's way of revealing a promise to the person having the dream.

Key - *The Bible denotes a key as an expression of one having been given access, and/or having a level of authority.*

"I will give you the keys of the kingdom of heaven; whatever you bind on earth will be bound in heaven, and whatever you loose on earth will be loosed in heaven.""
Matthew 16:19 NIV

Seeing a key in your dream, could indicate new opportunities in which you now have the grace and have been prepared enough to now access this opportunity. This new access may come in the form of a new opportunity in the dreamer's life.

For example, maybe someone once had difficulty growing their business because of lack of visibility. The key in the dream might represent an opportunity that would now allow them to receive the marketing and visibility that they didn't have prior.

Receiving a key in the dream may also signify the dreamer's spiritual maturity, with the Lord revealing their authority as a believer in Christ to "cast out demons," "heal the sick," "preach the gospel," and "cure diseases," as outlined in Luke 9:1-2.

Ladder - When dreaming of a ladder, you want to pay attention to specific details. Are you climbing upward? If so, this represents promotion and even being elevated naturally, spiritually, and emotionally. The concept is similar if the dreamer is going downward on the ladder. This would be an indicator that the dreamers' habits and decisions are causing them to experience demotion, failure, setback, and may be a warning that a person may becoming spiritually and emotionally dull.

 Another reference of a ladder/ stairway is in the Bible when Jacob had a dream and, in this vision, he observed a stairway connected to the heavens. He witnessed angels ascending and descending on the ladder. (Genesis 28:10-15) This was a divine encounter where the presence of the Lord was revealed to the dreamer.

License- The driver's license or identification card speaks on the dreamer's identity. Carrying your license indicates that you're in alignment with your identity in Christ and are on track with operating in your divine assignment.

 If this is a case where your license/Id card was stolen or is lost, it speaks on the enemy's assignment to keep you from realizing your full potential, so that you as the dreamer will never operate in your God ordained purpose. This dream is to warn the individual to be confident in what the Lord called you to do and to not allow insecurities, procrastination, etc to hinder you from walking in your purpose.

Microphone- *The dream involving the image of the microphone is to emphasize the need for the dreamer to speak. Proverbs 18:21 tells us that "Life and death are in the power of the tongue, and those who love it shall eat it's fruit." Begin to prophesy over yourself by speaking life and victory. The microphone can also indicate the Lord's plan to amplify the voice of the dreamer.*

Oil - *Oil is symbolic as being the anointing of the Lord. Olive oil specifically was traditionally used to anoint the Kings and Prophets to be commissioned into their perspective offices. "Then Samuel took a flask of olive oil and poured it on Saul's head and kissed him, saying, "Has not the Lord anointed you ruler over his inheritance?"*
(1 Samuel 10:1 NIV)

Additionally, anointing oil is recommended for use in praying for the sick, as stated in James 5:14-15: "Is anyone among you sick? Let them call the elders of the church to pray over them and anoint them with oil in the name of the Lord."

Phone - *The symbolism of a phone implies the need for communication. If your phone is missing, it suggests the urgent need for prayer. If you were on the phone talking, especially if you recall the conversation, the Lord may be highlighting that specific information for you to address.*

Purse - *The purse or wallet symbolizes valuables and the dreamer's provisions. This symbolism is reflected in scripture, particularly in the book of Haggai. The people of that time faced consequences for prioritizing their needs over the Lord's, emphasizing the importance of putting God first.*

 "Now this is what the Lord Almighty says: 'Give careful thought to your ways. You have planted much, but harvested little. You eat, but never have enough. You drink, but never have your fill. You put on clothes, but are not warm. You earn wages, only to put them in a purse with holes in it.'"
 (Haggai 1:5-6 NIV)

Rainbow - *The rainbow symbolizes the promises of God and His covenant with the dreamer. This dream is the Lord's way of providing comfort and assuring the dreamer of His promises.*

 "I have set my rainbow in the clouds, and it will be the sign of the covenant between me and the earth."
~Genesis 9:13

Rock - *The Bible references the rock multiple times as representing our Lord Jesus. In 2 Samuel 22:47, it says, "The Lord lives! Praise be to my Rock! Exalted be my God, the Rock, my Savior!" The rock also signifies being firmly planted in God's Word and submitted to His ways. "And I tell you that you are Peter, and on this rock, I will build my church, and the gates of Hades will not overcome it." (Matthew 16:18 NIV)*

Stage- If the dreamer finds themselves on stage, it reveals the level of influence they are called to walk in. The stage highlights the authority and influence the dreamer will carry, bringing insight into their purpose. If the experience on the stage is displeasing or unsettling, the dreamer should take inventory and be aware of any negative occurrences or character flaws that could sabotage their reputation as a person of influence.

Sword- Seeing the sword in a dream is symbolic of the word of God. The scripture mentions in Ephesians 6:17:
 "Take the helmet of salvation and the sword of the Spirit, which is the word of God."

 The sword in a dream is an expression of the word of God needing to be used as the weapon against your adversary.

Table- This symbol signifies the place where decisions and negotiations are made. The Lord could be "preparing your table" in the presence of your enemies, referencing the blessing you will publicly receive. The table is also where you eat and receive your "spiritual food," like the word of God. For example, sitting at a table with your pastor represents receiving teaching from this leader. Pay attention to who's at the table with you to verify if this is someone you can trust for wisdom.

Window - When it comes to seeing a window in your dream, these messages are very much prophetic, aiming to get the dreamer to pay attention to what's being shown in the window. The Lord's purpose is to bring insight into a situation, place, person, or thing. Take note of what's being shown in the window as it's meant to provide a deeper revelation.

CHAPTER 5: PEOPLE

In this upcoming chapter, we will explore the most common individuals one might encounter in their dreams. These examples aim to help the reader understand the biblical significance of what each person may represent. It's crucial to note that when encountering people in dreams, the focus is not always on them literally but rather on what they symbolize to the dreamer. For instance,

I once dreamt of my sister, a flight attendant, aiding me in reaching my destination. In this instance, the Lord conveyed a message to me about forthcoming promotion and elevation. Her occupation was significant, explaining why she appeared in the dream.

As you navigate through this list in relation to your own dreams, please be aware that these interpretations are not universally precise for every person or dream. The entries in this chapter offer a guide to assist you, drawing on the most common meanings of these symbols.

Angels-*Encountering an angel in a dream is a frequent experience for believers in Christ Jesus. These divine interactions involve messengers of the Lord, dispatched directly to the individual to convey revelation, healing, provision, and more. In Genesis 18, three angels visited Abraham, described in the Bible as "men." "Abraham looked up and saw three men standing nearby" (Genesis 18:2). These men delivered a message to Abraham. Similarly, the dreamer may come across an angel appearing as a man or woman, assisting them or conveying important information.*

Army *- An army of troops in a dream can symbolize divine assistance from the Lord, indicating that the dreamer may be facing warfare or hardships. The presence of the army signifies God sending help. "Who is able to count his heavenly army? Doesn't his light shine on all the earth?" (Job 25:3 NLT). Conversely, an army opposing the believer could represent numerous challenges in the dreamer's life.*

Baby- *A baby in a dream may symbolize the birth of new endeavors, such as a business, ministry, or project for the believer. Additionally, babies in dreams could represent "babes" in Christ, reflecting those who are less mature in the faith. "And I, brethren, could not speak to you as to spiritual people but as to carnal, as to babes in Christ." (1 Corinthians 3:1 NKJV)*

Bestfriend *- A best friend or a very close friend in a dream could symbolize the Holy Spirit interacting with the dreamer. The Bible describes the Holy Spirit as our advocate, supporting and teaching us. "But the Advocate, the Holy Spirit, whom the Father will send in my name, will teach you all things and will remind you of everything I have said to you." (John 14:26 NIV)*

Bus-driver- *A bus driver in a dream symbolizes one guiding the dreamer towards their purpose. This driver could represent angelic assistance or the Lord leading the dreamer to their destination. If the driver is a known person, that person may play a significant role in helping the dreamer achieve their goals.*

Celebrity *- A celebrity in a dream often signifies influence and status. If the dreamer is assisting or engaging with the celebrity, it may reveal the current or potential level of influence that the dreamer holds.*

Children *- Seeing children in a dream often symbolizes something related to "youth." Depending on the context, it may be a reminder to approach the Lord with childlike faith.*

"And he said: "Truly I tell you, unless you change and become like little children, you will never enter the kingdom of heaven. Therefore, whoever takes the lowly position of this child is the greatest in the kingdom of heaven." (Matthew 18:3-4 NIV)

If you see your own children, it could refer to them literally or symbolize aspects of their character.

Classmates-*This represents someone whom the dreamer considers a peer. This individual may be in a similar industry as the dreamer and would symbolize someone who has undergone a similar process of development in their respective industries*

Co-Worker- *The scripture mentions co-workers as those who help advance the gospel of Jesus: "For we are co-workers in God's service; you are God's field, God's building." (1 Corinthians 3:9, NIV) A co-worker in the dream of a believer would represent someone laboring in ministry tasks.*

Deceased - *A deceased person in the dream can symbolize what the dreamer remembers most about them or convey a divine message about the dreamer's bloodline, with the Lord offering revelation. However, frequent dreams of deceased people should be approached cautiously, as it might involve deception.*

The Bible teaches that the dead are not permitted to visit the living, as illustrated in Luke 16:19-31, where a deceased man sought to warn his living relatives but was forbidden by Jesus. Consulting with the dead is prohibited, and if a dead person appears in a dream, it's considered a "familiar spirit" that needs to be cast out according to Mark 3:15.

Doctor - *The Doctor in a dream could represent the manifestation of healing, through the power of the Holy Spirit.*

"How God anointed Jesus of Nazareth with the Holy Ghost and with power: who went about doing good, and healing all that were oppressed of the devil; for God was with him." - Acts 10:38 KJV

Driver - *The symbolism of the driver in the dream indicates who is in control. If the dreamer is driving, it signifies authority and control over a situation. On the other hand, being a passenger with someone else driving suggests that the driver holds influence over the dreamer's life and decisions.*

Enemies - *An enemy in your dream typically symbolizes the Lord's reference to the adversary, Satan. It's not specifically about the individual, but a representation of the unseen enemy we contend with. Encountering your enemy in the dream may serve as a warning to pray against the plans of the evil one.*

 "For our struggle is not against flesh and blood, but against the rulers, against the authorities, against the powers of this dark world and against the spiritual forces of evil in the heavenly realms."
Ephesians 6:12 NIV

Father- *Encountering a father figure in a dream typically represents God, our heavenly Father, conveying a message or signaling His nearness. Although there are instances where the dream may literally involve the dreamer's actual father, it's crucial to understand that most dreams are symbolic rather than literal.*

 2 Corinthians 6:18 NIV mentions, "I will be a Father to you, and you will be my sons and daughters, says the Lord Almighty."

Grandparents - *Grandparents in a dream symbolize the revelation of generational insight. As the patriarch and matriarch, they commonly represent the bloodline of the dreamer. Pay careful attention to the dream's details, as the Lord may be imparting information related to the dreamer's family.*

Jesus - Encountering Jesus in a dream signifies a real-time visitation from the Lord. It's not just a vision but a divine interaction. Many believers, including myself, have experienced these encounters, often bringing comfort, reassurance, and commissioning for kingdom purposes. In Acts 9, Saul's vision of Jesus halted his persecution of believers and led to his commissioning as an Apostle.

King - Dreaming of a king symbolizes status, great influence, and represents the Lord Jesus, our "king of kings" and "Lord of Lords" (Revelation 17:14). It serves as a message emphasizing Jesus' lordship and majesty, while also indicating the dreamer's potential for significant influence and notoriety in life.

Minister - This message could be timely from the Lord. Often, the words spoken by this minister are a manifestation of the Lord Himself being revealed through them.

Mom - Due to the nurturing and caring nature of a mother, observing your mom providing guidance and assistance in the dream is a manifestation of angelic and divine intervention. Often, the Lord utilizes someone trustworthy to the dreamer for instruction and comfort, which is why we may encounter our mother in a dream.

Neighbor - *The Bible emphasizes loving and treating neighbors with mercy and consideration. Romans 15:2 encourages believers to please their neighbors for their good, building them up. Additionally, Mark 12:31 instructs us to "Love your neighbor as yourself." Dreaming of a neighbor often indicates the importance of demonstrating love and mercy towards that individual.*

Passenger - *The passenger in the dream is symbolic of those who accompany the dreamer. Many times, the dreamer may see their children, a spouse, or some other loved one as a passenger. In this example, the message would be about the dreamer, but specifically as it relates to those individuals in the vehicle.*

Police- *Because of the authoritative nature of a police officer, they are symbolic for divine assistance from the Lord. Many people have testified to having dreams in which they're dialing "911" to contact the police. This is an instruction for the dreamer to pray and seek the urgent council of the Lord.*

Priests - *The Bible references the priest as Jesus, our high priest. "but because Jesus lives forever, he has a permanent priesthood." Hebrews 7:24 NIV*
Seeing a priest may represent the high priest, our Lord Jesus.

It could also be an encouraging reminder to the dreamer, letting them know that the Lord has chosen them and considers them valuable. "But you are a chosen people, a royal priesthood, a holy nation, God's special possession, that you may declare the praises of him who called you out of darkness into his wonderful light."
1 Peter 2:9 NIV

Relative *- It's common for the dreamer to receive divine insight about a family member. However, dreaming of a relative may signify the Lord's revelation about the dreamer's family, often with that trusted relative, being a symbol of angelic assistance.*

Sibling*- Seeing a brother or sister in a dream could refer to that person literally or symbolize the Lord speaking about Christians in general. Throughout scripture, believers in Christ are referred to as "brothers and sisters." Jesus emphasized this by stating, "My mother and brothers are those who hear God's word and put it into practice" (Luke 8:21 NIV)*

Spirits*- Often, the dreamer may encounter a spirit that doesn't resemble a human. Depending on the dream's context, this spirit could signify either an evil spirit or the Holy Spirit. Discernment is crucial for identifying the spirit's source. It's important to note that any spirit acting contrary to the teachings of the Bible is not the Holy Spirit.*

Spouse - *A spouse in the dream is symbolic of a covenant. It's not necessarily an indication of your spouse literally, but more about a covenant with either the Lord Jesus, another person, or entity.*

I had a dream several years ago when I gave my life to Christ. The Lord told me He was sending me a husband to feed me the word. In this dream, he wasn't talking about a literal husband, but about me being in covenant with a specific ministry.

Throughout scripture, the Lord also refers to his followers as "his bride". Jesus references his love and commitment for the body of believers, similar to the love of a loyal husband to his wife. Therefore, when a spouse is in a dream, It may represent the Lord's personal covenant with the dreamer.

Additionally, based on the context, seeing a spouse in the dream could reveal an evil entity that has been referred to incubus/succubus. These are wicked spirits known to make covenant with their victim by claiming that person as a spouse in the spiritual realm. They are usually the cause of hinderances in the dreamers' waking lives, many times causing interference in their victims' relationships and ability to have successful marriages, friendships, etc. Genesis 6:1-4 mentions the Nephilims which are fallen angels who married and had children with humans. If you discern that the spouse you saw in the dream may have been evil in nature, use this dream as an opportunity to pray against any evil spirit trying to claim you in the spiritual realm.

Stranger - *Strangers in a dream can embody either angels or demons. If these strangers are helpful and align with God's ways, it may indicate angelic assistance, as Hebrews 13:2 highlights the potential for entertaining angels unknowingly.*

Conversely, if the strangers exhibit wicked behavior or deception, it suggests the presence of a demonic spirit.

Teacher - *Teachers in a dream symbolize a period of testing or the need for preparation in various aspects of life, such as family, business, or ministry. The presence of teachers signifies the Lord's guidance, emphasizing the importance of readiness and study in the individual's journey.*

"God is exalted in his power. Who is a teacher like him?" - Job 36:22 NIV

CHAPTER 6: PLACES

Believers often encounter symbolic locations in their dreams, each with significant meanings. In this chapter, we'll explore common dream locations, emphasizing the importance of understanding biblical references and general significance. For instance, working at a fire station may suggest a grace for conflict resolution and extinguishing chaos in others' lives. This guide aims to provide clarity and deeper insights into the meanings of your dreams.

Airport -_The airport serves as a preparatory ground for the dreamer, signaling forthcoming promotion and elevation in a specific aspect of their life. It signifies proximity to an opportunity and conveys a message that a favorable chance is on the horizon._

Basement_- The basement of a home symbolizes concealed secrets, suppressed memories, and underlying concerns. The message underscores the importance of addressing issues stored in the dreamer's subconscious, bringing them into awareness._

Bathroom _- The bathroom is symbolic of deliverance and salvation, with the shower representing the cleansing of sin, as stated in Psalms 51:2 (NIV): "Wash away all my iniquity and cleanse me from my sin." If someone is in the bathroom, it implies they are undergoing a form of deliverance in a specific area of their life._

Bedroom _- This is the place where deeper revelation and insight is being given to the dreamer. It represents a place of comfort, rest, and covenant._

Cave - A cave is symbolic for isolation or separation. Throughout scripture, a cave was mentioned as being a hiding place for protection or a place of burial or seclusion.

 "When the Israelites saw that their situation was critical and that their army was hard pressed, they hid in caves and thickets, among the rocks, and in pits and cisterns."
(1 Samuel 13:6 NIV)

 The message of this dream would illustrate that either the Lord is advising of some separation or consecration that may be needed. It could also reveal an agenda of the enemy to cause the individual to isolate and become less sociable, to their detriment.

Church - The church represents holiness, purity, and the presence of God. It represents the place of worship, the body of Christ, and/or the Kingdom of Heaven. The context of the dream where a church is seen is important, as that would indicate what the message is truly revealing to the dreamer.

 It may be a message to advise that prayer and fellowship is needed for the dreamer. It could also be a message speaking about Christianity as a whole.

Childhood-home- A childhood home in a dream speaks of past events in the dreamer's childhood that may impact their present life. It could also indicate generational messages related to the individual's family. Constantly dreaming of the former home may represent setbacks and delays in the dreamer's life.

Classroom- *If you find yourself in a classroom, this is an indication that studying is needed or that it's a time of preparation in the dreamer's life.*

Closet - *The closet is a representation of a secret place. This symbol reveals the secret matters of the hearts. It may also be a message advising the dreamer that intimacy in prayer is needed. Jesus mentioned in the KJV of Matthew 6:6: "But thou, when thou prayest, enter into thy closet, and when thou hast shut thy door, pray to thy Father which is in secret; and thy Father which seeth in secret shall reward thee openly."*

Downstairs- *This represents demotion or even failure. Going downstairs can also reference the dreamer's spiritual status. This could be an indication for the dreamer to have more intimacy with God and even the importance of studying the word.*

Farm - *A farm is symbolic of provision and resources. In biblical and agricultural history, the crops produced from a farm indicated riches and abundance, representing financial status and the fulfillment of needs.*

"You and your sons and your servants are to farm the land for him and bring in the crops so that your master's grandson may be provided for." - 2 Samuel 9:10 NIV

Funeral- *A funeral indicates the death or finality of something, more symbolic than literal. For example, the Bible speaks of death as something believers should do daily, encouraging us to die to self in order to live.*

"He himself bore our sins in his body on the cross, so that we might die to sins and live for righteousness; by his wounds, you have been healed." - 1 Peter 2:24 NIV

Forest- *The beauty of the forest and the greenery is symbolic of abundant provision, prosperity, and peace.*

"The Lord is my shepherd, I lack nothing. He makes me lie down in green pastures, he leads me beside quiet waters, he refreshes my soul." (Psalm 23:1-2 NIV)

Garage- *A garage symbolizes a place of stillness and complacency concerning the pursuit of specific goals and accomplishments. If there's a vehicle parked in the garage or if the dreamer is spending time there, it could be a warning against procrastination.*

Garden - *The symbolism of the garden can represent a land of plentiful, prosperity, and promise. Depending on the context of the dream, if there's an enemy in the garden, it could mean to pay attention to deception that could affect the life of the dreamer.*

"Build houses and settle down; plant gardens and eat what they produce."
Jeremiah 29:5 NIV

"Now the serpent was more crafty than any of the wild animals the Lord God had made. He said to the woman, "Did God really say, 'You must not eat from any tree in the garden'?""- Genesis 3:1 NIV

Gas-Station - *Being at a gas station, whether filling up a vehicle with gas or attending to other preparations like putting air in a tire, symbolizes receiving the necessary resources for the journey ahead. These resources could be tangible or informational, aiding the dreamer in moving forward.*

Home- *Dreams involving homes can symbolize individuals, the body of Christ, a family, a church, or a ministry. Identifying the owner of the home is crucial, as the message is significant to the owner of that home.*

Hospital- *The symbolism of the hospital is compared to the church. The Lord made a statement in scripture: "Jesus said to them, "It is not the healthy who need a doctor, but the sick. I have not come to call the righteous, but sinners."- Mark 2:17 NIV*

This might symbolize someone who isn't well and in need of healing. It could signify a person requiring urgent assistance, along with the need for deliverance and salvation.

Hotel - *A hotel often symbolizes a temporary place or season in an individual's life. This dream may suggest a period of transition for the dreamer, indicating shifts in career, financial status, or personal life. It signals a message that the current experiences, whether present or upcoming, are transient and not permanent. The dreamer is advised not to grow too comfortable in this phase, as it's a passing process.*

Kitchen- *The kitchen is the place where we eat. It's the place where food is being prepared. The kitchen is symbolic of spiritual food. The Lord Jesus references himself as the living bread. He's instructed believers in him to receive the bread of life, which is the word of God. "For the bread of God is the bread that comes down from heaven and gives life to the world."(John 6:33 NIV)*

Therefore, when dreaming of a kitchen, it could represent the ministry in which the dreamer attends. It could symbolize the minister or pastor that the dreamer receives the word of God from. It can also symbolize the need for the individual to receive the word of God.

Lake- *The sight of a lake in a dream symbolizes the presence of the Holy Spirit. If the waters are clear, creating a serene and peaceful scene, it serves as a reminder to the dreamer of the Lord's presence and encourages confidence.*

"Shortly before dawn Jesus went out to them, walking on the lake." ~Matthew 14:25 NIV

Additionally, the meaning of the lake can be inferred from its appearance. For instance, if the lake's waters are clear, it signifies a smooth journey, whereas muddy waters suggest challenging situations in the individual's life.

Livingroom - *The living room, also referred to as the family room, indicates family-related matters or concerns in the dream. The dreamer should take note and consider what the Lord might be unveiling regarding their family. Observing the individuals present in this scene can offer insights into specific details related to the dreamer's family.*

Mountain- *The mountain signifies either an obstacle or hindrance, as referenced in Mark 11:23: "Truly I tell you, if anyone says to this mountain, 'Go, throw yourself into the sea,' and does not doubt in their heart but believes that what they say will happen, it will be done for them." Additionally, a mountain may symbolize a high place of honor, whether in a natural or spiritual context, as stated in Psalms 2:6: "I have installed my king on Zion, my holy mountain."*

Office- *Dreaming of an office is symbolic of a job, entrepreneurship, or even a ministry. The message typically offers the dreamer insight into one of these areas. What is the dreamer doing in the office? Whether leading meetings or sitting at the table among influential people, this message could suggest that the dreamer is called to leadership in some capacity.*

Outside - Dreams that take place outside can have various meanings. For instance, on a beautiful sunny day, the dream's details could symbolize positive experiences. Conversely, if it's dark outside, it may represent a season of trials and the presence of evil.

 "As long as it is day, we must do the works of him who sent me. Night is coming, when no one can work. While I am in the world, I am the light of the world." -John 9:4-5 NIV

Porch - The porch is the part of a person's life or personality that's visible for others to see. The porch also symbolizes the foundation of the individual. Are you on a firm and solid foundation? Are you on a shaky foundation that can be destroyed based on unfortunate experiences in life?

 "The rain came down, the streams rose, and the winds blew and beat against that house; yet it did not fall, because it had its foundation on the rock."
 Matthew 7:25 NIV

Prison - The prison is a place of bondage, captivity, and illustrates limitations in the life of the dreamer or of the person whose confined in the prison.

 "You brought us into prison and laid burdens on our backs."
 Psalms 66:11 NIV

Store - *The store is an indication of provision and resources. "The Lord will open the heavens, the storehouse of his bounty, to send rain on your land in season and to bless all the work of your hands. You will lend to many nations but will borrow from none." ~Deuteronomy 28:12 NIV*

Stadium - *The stadium is a symbol of great influence and the Lord amplifying the voice of the dreamer.*

Upstairs - *Going upstairs in a dream, represents elevation and promotion. The promotion could be natural or even a spiritual ascension, where an individual is growing higher in the ways of the Lord.*

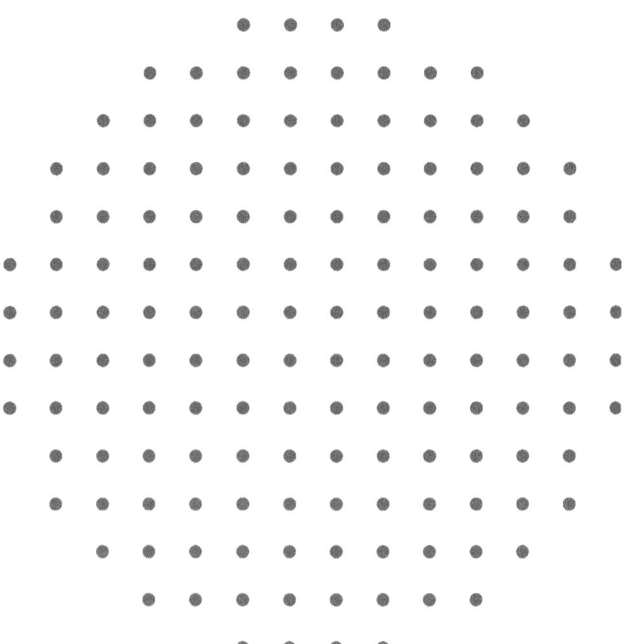

CHAPTER 7-
EXPERIENCES AND DECEPTION IN DREAMS:

Understanding that the Lord communicates through our dreams, it's crucial to recognize that our adversary seeks to plant evil and project demonic agendas as we sleep. A relevant parable, discussed by Jesus in Matthew 13, is the Parable of the Weeds. "The kingdom of heaven is like a man who sowed good seed in his field. But while everyone was sleeping, his enemy came and sowed weeds among the wheat, and went away. When the wheat sprouted and formed heads, then the weeds also appeared. 'Sir, didn't you sow good seed in your field? Where then did the weeds come from?' 'An enemy did this,' he replied." (Matthew 13:24-28 NIV)

In this parable, Jesus emphasizes that while people are asleep, the enemy plants evil intent. It underscores the importance of paying attention to dreams to discern potential weapons the enemy forms against you and pray effectively. Due to the enemy's craftiness, seek the Lord's spirit of wisdom and the gift of discernment (1 Corinthians 12:8-10). The enemy can be deceptive in dreams, presenting seemingly harmless images masking evil agendas. Even in dream Interpretation, while previous chapters provide common interpretations, be cautious not to solely rely on them. The enemy may misuse such information to deceive. For instance, the Lord may use a dream with a trusted loved one to convey a timely message, but lack of discernment could let the enemy exploit that trust to lead you into a detrimental covenant.

Praying and seeking the counsel of the Lord is crucial to avoid deception. Knowing and consistently meditating on God's Word is vital, as the Lord never contradicts His scriptures. Deception, often present in dreams, traces back to the enemy's tactics seen in Genesis 3, where Satan deceived Eve, leading to a curse. The serpent still deceives today, using false dreams, visions, and messages that mimic the Holy Spirit but originate from demons. Many have been led away from the faith due to this deception. The "angel of light" (the enemy) cunningly draws people from the truth, diverting them from their divine destiny.

Many individuals have encountered events in dreams that serve as "red flags" signaling potential deception or the workings of witchcraft. The dreamer's lack of awareness allows the enemy to succeed in executing its plan.

Examples of experiences revealing hidden agendas include:

- **_Eating in dreams._** _(Regrettably, witches have often succeeded in practicing witchcraft covertly by astral projecting into dreams through the spirit realm and feeding their victim. This act is essentially a charm concocted to harm the individual.)_

- **_Having Sex/Kissing_**_. (Especially as a single, non-married person. This is the result of a demon/marine spirit/spirit spouse attempting to forge an evil covenant with the dreamer to fulfill its wicked intent.)_

- **_Going through a maze or always coming to a roadblock_** _(This is an indication of some sort of curse of hindrance and limitation that's already in operation in the dreamer's life, or an attempt by the enemy to bring stagnation and hindrance.)_

- ·**_Walking or driving in the dark_**_. (It's an indication of dark times, hardship, warfare, or the enemy attempting to "keep you in the dark," in a low place, in a place of uncertainty.)_

- **_Things being stolen from you in the dream_**_. (The enemy comes to steal, kill, and destroy; therefore, this is an indication of the enemy trying to steal something from you, based on what was taken in the dream.)_

- **_Signing contracts or giving money_**_. (Please be discerning; this isn't always the case, but many times it's the enemy trying to lure the dreamer into signing a contract and agreeing with a curse through gaining a signature or a sacrifice, which is the money through the spirit realm, so that the plans of the enemy would function in the life of the victim.)_

- **_Being in prison or chains_**. *(This indicates some level of bondage in the life of the individual.)*

- **_Running or being chased_**. *(This is a spirit of fear and intimidation trying to pursue the dreamer and operate through their life. Take authority and command that spirit to leave you in Jesus' name.)*

These are just a few examples of how deception may manifest in dreams. It's crucial to understand that the Word of God assures us that, as believers redeemed by the blood of Jesus Christ, "no weapon formed against us shall prosper" (Isaiah 54:17). We possess authority over all the power of the enemy, and nothing by any means shall harm us (Luke 10:19). Therefore, if you encounter any of these dreams and discern that the enemy has sought to bring harm to you, stand firm, declare the Word of the Lord, and rebuke the enemy. Nullify any schemes the enemy has devised against you.

It's crucial to recall that regardless of any curse, hex, vex, incantation, generational bondage, or evil assignment the enemy may attempt in your life, the Word assures us that Christ Jesus has redeemed us from every curse. This means that when we repent of our sins and are in right standing with the Lord, we can use the Word of the Lord to renounce and cancel any curse. "Christ redeemed us from the curse of the law by becoming a curse for us, for it is written: 'Cursed is everyone who is hung on a pole.' He redeemed us in order that the blessing given to Abraham might come to the Gentiles through Christ Jesus, so that by faith we might receive the promise of the Spirit."
Galatians 3:13-14 NIV

Regardless of what you encounter, stand confidently in the Lord, in His Word, and His promises. Fear not, for as a believer and follower of Christ, the Lord God is with you and will fight for you. He "hasn't given us a spirit of fear, but of love, power, and a sound mind" (2 Timothy 1:7). You don't have to accept those evil dreams and wicked plans. Upon waking up, cancel the dreams and the evil intent, plead the blood of Jesus over you, and stand firm on the Word of God. Do not go back to sleep without rebuking the enemy's intent and praying the perfect will of the Heavenly Father, in Jesus' name.

Deliverance Prayers

In this next section, I've provided a template of prayers that can be recited upon waking up from your dream. Are you required to pray these prayers to get the Lord to intervene? Absolutely not! However, the Word says that "whatever you bind on Earth will be bound in heaven, and whatever you loose on Earth will be loosed in heaven" (Matthew 18:18). Why did the Lord give us this instruction if deliverance is automatic when we are in Christ? This is because, although deliverance is promised and has been purchased through the powerful blood of Jesus Christ, we have to use our words to continue to enforce our freedom, the promises of the Lord, and bind every enemy who would attempt to bind us.

If you find yourself waking up out of a dream that you discern was demonically engineered, even if you aren't fully certain what the dream meant, I encourage you to pray the following prayers.

Prayer and Decrees to destroy evil covenants & altars:

Repent: "Father, in the name of Jesus, I ask that you forgive me for every known and unknown sin I've committed, including the sins committed by my bloodline against you Lord. I ask that you extend us mercy and cleanse us from every unrighteousness. I thank you Lord for your promise to forgive me according to 1 John 1:9."

Every covenant and initiation Made in the natural realm or in a dream -

To witchcraft and rebellion, which is witchcraft, to idolatry, which is witchcraft, or in ANY way where the enemy tried to initiate me into witchcraft, I hereby RENOUNCE this sin, I denounce witchcraft. I hereby withdraw my membership to witchcraft, by reason of the blood covenant of Jesus which speaks greater things than any evil blood that may be crying out against me.

Every covenant and initiation Made in the natural realm or in a dream

To bring pre-mature death, murder, infirmity, and even aborted destiny in my life or the life of my kid(s)/family, I renounce you and CANCEL your assignment against us. I withdraw EVERY vow made knowingly or unknowingly to agree with death, sickness, or aborted destinies. May every demonic contract tying my life to death be Nullified NOW!

Every covenant and initiation Made in the natural realm or in a dream

To the marine kingdom and to a spirit spouse/mate be cancelled now according to the law of the Lord in Numbers 30, that declares that any covenant I made that the Father doesn't approve of will be nullified. By reason of the powerful blood of Jesus, I destroy every covenant with your wicked kingdom, whether made by me or my ancestors. I destroy the agreement and divorce myself from every covenant of evil intent, including those that would try to bring anti-marriage in my life.

I cancel every assignment from this wicked kingdom that would attempt block and hinder my earthly marriage. I come against the spirit of rejection, I will not be rejected nor hidden from the God ordained relationships and destiny helpers assigned by the Lord.

Every covenant and initiation made in the natural realm or in a dream

To bring calamity, chaos, failure, disaster, backwardness, destruction, anti-progress, anti-success, your assignment is terminated! Your contract is hereby revoked. By reason of the blood covenant of Jesus, who sacrificed himself for me, so that I would NEVER have to live under a curse, but that I would have life and have it more abundantly; I demand sabotaging spirits to leave NOW! Every covenant of hardship, misfortune, failure, constant disappointment, insufficiency, never having enough, lack, delay- your assignment is Finished! You are hereby terminated. I renounce your legal right to operate in my life or my kids/family's life. My covenant with you is hereby terminated. I replace this curse with a blessing of the Lord that "maketh rich and add no sorrow" (Proverbs 10:22).

I replace it with the word that says, I'm blessed when I come in, and blessed when I go out. (Deuteronomy 28:6). I replace every curse with the blessing of Abraham. Since I am an heir of my forefather Abraham, I receive my inheritance.

Every covenant and initiation Made in the natural realm or in a dream

By me or another individual, that invited demons/evil spirits/unclean spirits/all forms of darkness- into my home or any place I rest- or any place my kid(s)/family rest, by reason of the blood of Jesus, and the Law of the Lord from Numbers 30-that wicked contract is revoked. I evict you evil spirits from our lives and our home. The blood of Jesus blots out every evil ordinance already written against my name and my kid(s)/family's name. I command every evil spirit- to leave our lives NOW! I take authority over you- you will come no more. I unyoke myself from you with the blood of Jesus.

May the angels of the Lord drive away every evil entity, that would still attempt to claim my life, my child's life, or my family.

Every covenant and initiation Made in the natural realm or in a dream

With the kingdom of darkness, I now sever EVERY one of these covenants with Satan and the kingdom of darkness that gave evil spirits permission to follow and monitor my life, my kid's life, or my family's life and progress, you will follow us nor monitor us anymore! I shred your contract and divorce myself from this covenant, regardless of how the covenant was made. I revoke ANY consent with you Satan, and by reason of the blood of Jesus-I'm no longer obligated by this contract. I return any "gift" that I may have received from your kingdom, even if unknowingly.

I renounce this agreement. I'm now in a NEW covenant, which is with the Father-Son-Holy Spirit, who already purchased me with the blood of Jesus. I am Free and Free indeed! You evil spirit, I command you to leave and never return.

Every covenant and initiation Made in the natural realm or in a dream

With any ancestral powers, curses, or evil hereditary traits from my bloodline on both my father and mother side-I renounce your assignment against my life, my kid(s) life, and my family. I even pray for my kid(s) and sever any bloodline curses and evil covenants against their life that may be in force as a result of their other parent's bloodline. I command it to be cancelled now, by reason of the blood covenant of Jesus and the mercy of the Lord. Every ancestral curse and evil covenant set up to propel our lives to the same type of deception, failure, poverty, etc—or that would attempt to control and destroy our lives, destiny, & the Lord's perfect will for us —May this covenant be destroyed now! I hereby withdraw my membership and renounce my agreement to ancestral curses and evil covenants that would seek to "tie up" my life to the same failures of my ancestors. You are hereby terminated!

I pray this prayer by faith and seal these decrees in the name of the Father, Son- Jesus, and in the power of Holy Spirit.

Prayers against evil altars:

- •May every EVIL altar speaking against me and my family be destroyed by the FIRE of the Lord.

- I dismantle and destroy every evil sacrifice made on a witch altar that's crying out against my name—-be annihilated!

- May the God who answers by fire come down- the same way my fore-Father Elijah called down fire from heaven in 2Kings 1, Lord God, cause a Holy Ghost fire to fall on and destroy every evil altar and it's sacrifice and dedication that was sent against me and my family.

- I strip down every dedication on these evil altars and hereby cut the cord, that allowed witches to hire demons to harass me or my family.

- May the angels of the Lord per psalm 91, be released to visit every place where there's an evil altar raised against me, my children, and my family. May the angels of the Lord remove any objects/details/residue that's connecting us to these altars.

- Lord your word says in Exodus 22:18 to "suffer not a witch to live". According to your own word Lord, may any un-repented witch, seeking to kill and destroy me, my kid(s), my family- may they be condemned by their own words, according to Isaiah 54:17. For your word says that no weapon formed against me shall prosper, and every tongue that rises against me in judgement is condemned.

- *Lord, the same way you sent a death angel to block the path of Balaam, a sorcery who was hired to curse your children-May you do the same for me Lord. Block the path of every enemy who would attempt to curse me, my kid(s), or my family, in Jesus' name.*

- *Heavenly Father, I thank you that you hear me and that you always hear me. May you be glorified and exalted. Thank you for honoring my word, Lord. May you order my steps, each day. May my life be a continuous sabbath rest, where I'm always "rested" in you Lord, no matter the circumstance. May I experience your perfect shalom in every area of my life, nothing missing, nothing broken, nothing lacking, in Jesus' name. May goodness and mercy follow me and my family all the days of our long, healthy, prosperous life. In the almighty name of Jesus, Amen.*

Overview

I pray that this book and the teaching have allowed you to receive clarity and wisdom concerning the language of Heaven through dreams and visions. Please be advised that there is absolutely no book that replaces the importance of us studying the written word of the Lord through our Bible. This is how we can effectively "test every spirit" and teaching and not be deceived by every doctrine. This is also how we can reference our dreams so that we aren't led deceptively.

I am grateful and blessed for the Lord God allowing me the privilege to teach on such a topic and to serve the Kingdom of Heaven by allowing my brothers and sisters in Christ Jesus to become more aware of the voice of the Lord and to perceive His instructions. Moreover, I am thankful for the opportunity to equip every reader, to stand and wage a good warfare against the adversary.

If you are reading this book, I want to say thank you. May the Lord bless you and keep you. May he make His face shine upon you and be gracious towards you. May the Lord impart a fresh level of grace unto you. May he increase you with more of His wisdom and insight, in Jesus' name. My request of you is that you would pray for me as well, that the Lord would continue to bless and protect my family and I, as we do the work of our Lord and savior Jesus Christ and that his perfect will shall be established in my life. In Jesus name.

Dream Journal:

Dream Journal:

Dream Journal:

Dream Journal:

Dream Journal:

Dream Journal:

Dream Journal:

Dream Journal:

Dream Journal:

Dream Journal:

Dream Journal:

Dream Journal:

Dream Journal:

Dream Journal:

Dream Journal:

Dream Journal:

Dream Journal:

Dream Journal:

Dream Journal:

Dream Journal:

Dream Journal:

Dream Journal:

Dream Journal:

Dream Journal:

Dream Journal:

Dream Journal:

Dream Journal:

Dream Journal:

Dream Journal:

Dream Journal:

Dream Journal:

Dream Journal:

Dream Journal:

Dream Journal:

Dream Journal:

Dream Journal:

Dream Journal:

Dream Journal:

Dream Journal:

Dream Journal:

Dream Journal:

Dream Journal:

Dream Journal:

Dream Journal:

Dream Journal:

Dream Journal:

Dream Journal:

Dream Journal:

Dream Journal:

Dream Journal:

Dream Journal:

Dream Journal:

Dream Journal:

Dream Journal:

Dream Journal:

Dream Journal:

Dream Journal:

Dream Journal:

Dream Journal:

Dream Journal:

Dream Journal: